A Pocket Guide to the Anglican Church

by

RONALD H. LLOYD

Precentor of Christ Church, Oxford,
formerly Chaplain of the Dragon School, Oxford

MOWBRAY
LONDON & OXFORD

First published 1980 under the title *After Confirmation*, now
revised and published in paperback 1984 by
A. R. Mowbray & Co. Ltd,
Saint Thomas House, Becket Street, Oxford, OX1 1SJ

ISBN 0 264 66996 7

Typeset by Oxford Publishing Services

CONTENTS

ACKNOWLEDGEMENTS

Acknowledgement is gratefully made to: William Barclay (*Epilogues and Prayers*); J. S. Hoyland; R. K. Ingram (*Hymns and Prayers for Dragons*); David Ingram; D. M. Prescott (*Senior Teachers Assembly Book*); Alison White (*Retreats*)

FOREWORD

by the Rt Revd Patrick Rodger, Bishop of Oxford

What many Christians want (and not only when they are young, either) is solid information about their faith and about the life of the Church — not just pious generalities. They are also eager to find prayers that they can use often and come to love, such as will nourish their own halting attempts at prayer.

Both of the above are to be found in this booklet which I am happy to commend, especially for the use of candidates for Confirmation. Ronald Lloyd is thoroughly experienced in pastoral ministry to adults, young people and children alike. In a way that is at once crisp and friendly, he has put a great deal of knowledge in a small compass at the service of them all.

November 1983   †Patrick Oxon

Membership of the Church

When we were baptized we were united with Christ. In most cases, however, we were baptized in infancy when we had no say in the matter.

Confirmation gives us the opportunity of declaring publicly in the presence of the gathered Church our decision to follow Jesus Christ.

It gives us the opportunity of making our own promises to God.

It gives us the full rights of membership in the Church which enable us to participate actively in the priesthood of Christ.

'Come, and let yourselves be built, as living stones, into a spiritual temple; become a holy priesthood, to offer spiritual sacrifices acceptable to God through Jesus Christ'. (I Peter 2. 5)

This means that all baptized people are strictly speaking priests in virtue of their membership in the priestly body of Christ.

But what does this mean?

The answer lies in the term 'priest' and its definition. The Latin word for priest is 'pontifex' which means 'bridge builder'. A priest is one who builds a bridge between man and God. That is the role of the confirmed Christian.

The Catholic Church

The word *catholic* comes from a Greek word meaning 'universal'. The Anglican Church is a part of the Catholic Church because Anglicans believe that:

(i) The Holy Scriptures of the Old and New Testaments contain all things necessary for salvation and are the rule and ultimate standard of faith.

(ii) The way we interpret the Scriptures must in no way contradict any statement contained in the Apostles' Creed and the Nicene Creed.

(iii) There are two sacraments necessary for salvation, namely Baptism and Holy Communion.

(iv) There are three orders of ministry, namely, Bishop, Priest and Deacon.

A Rule of Life

1. To pray every day.

Praying is conversing and keeping company with God. There are different kinds of prayer.

Thanksgiving: When we thank God for all his blessings.

Confession: When we admit our faults before God and ask for pardon.

Intercession: When we pray for the needs of others.

Petition: When we bring before God our own requests.

Meditation: When we give God a chance of talking to us. The ideal way of doing this is to read a section from the Gospel and then try to think it through.

Adoration: When we surrender our love to God in response to his love for us.

Clearly to cover so much ground takes time, and so often we find that time is a limited commodity. However, we must never rush our prayers by trying to cover the ground in the time available. It may therefore be more rewarding if we can set aside certain moments of the day when we can concentrate our thoughts on a particular aspect of prayer, e.g.

Early morning: *Thanksgiving* for sleep, for another day, for family, for friends, for the beauty of the earth.

Middle day: *Intercession* for others, especially those in need and distress.

Afternoon: *Petition* for our own needs and problems.

Evening: *Confession* of our sins, and in true penitence asking for God's forgiveness.

| Late evening: | *Meditation* on a short passage of the Bible letting God speak to us. |
| Any moment: | *Adoration* of God in loving response to his presence. |

2. To behave towards others as we would like others to behave towards us, even at the expense of our own convenience, and not expecting any return.

3. To be regular in attendance at Church. To partake of the Blessed Sacrament and to hear the Word of God expounded. Ideally we should do this every Sunday as it is our holy day.

4. To be constant in our witness of Christ. Far too often Christians remain silent when they should stand up and be recognized. Someone once said, 'Show me that you are redeemed and I will believe in your Redeemer'.

5. To be generous towards God with our money and our time.

6. To read our Bible every day to discover the 'Word' of God. Ideally we should read our Bibles with the help of a commentary. Your parish priest will advise you on this.

The Purpose of Life

The purpose of life lies in the quality of relationships.

Our relationship with God:

To live our lives ever conscious of the fact that we are in God's presence.

Our relationships with people:

To remember that each person is a child of God and should be treated with the love and respect that Jesus himself always showed to a fellow being.

Our relationships with all God's creatures:

To safeguard at all times a creature's life and dignity, and protect it from suffering and pain.

Our relationship with the earth:

To play our part, however small, in caring for the environment around us, the land, the waters and the atmosphere.

Life after Death

A Christian believes that:

We come from God and we go to God.

This life is a preparation for eternal life.

Through baptism we enter the spiritual world and experience it in prayer, worship, mutual service and love. This experience, however, is limited by our physical nature. When the physical body dies we will enter fully into the spiritual world and experience it without any limitation. St Paul tells us, 'My knowledge now is partial; then it will be whole, like God's knowledge of me'. (I Corinthians 13.12)

As God has clothed us with a physical body for living in this world, so he will clothe us with a spiritual body for living in the next. St Paul puts it this way, 'As we have worn the likeness of the man made of dust, so we shall wear the likeness of the heavenly man . . . This perishable being must be clothed with the imperishable, and what is mortal must be clothed with immortality'. (I Corinthians 15. 49, 53)

We shall retain our own individual identities. You will still be you, I will still be me, and we will recognize one another. Loves and friendships enjoyed here on earth will continue in the next life. Jesus whilst hanging on the cross emphasized this when he said to the thief, 'I tell you this: today *you* shall be with *me* in Paradise'. (St Luke 23. 43)

Each one of us will be required to stand before the throne of God on the Day of Judgement to render an account of the way we have lived our lives whilst here on earth.

The Bible

The first step towards an understanding of the Bible is to realize that it is not one book but many. It is a library of writings covering a period of about a thousand years. These writings fall into two main divisions, the Old Testament and the New Testament.

The books of the New Testament were written over the course of about one hundred years, and mainly consist of the letters of a busy missionary (the letters of St Paul), the travel diary of a doctor (the Book of Acts), and the sayings of Jesus linked to his birth, ministry, death and resurrection (the Gospel according to Matthew, Mark, Luke and John).

The books of the Old Testament are quite different in character and were written over a period of some eight or nine hundred years. These books represent the surviving national literature of Israel and vary considerably one from the other.

A brief comparison with our own national literature may help us to understand this better.

Suppose we could bind together under one cover the chief literature of the English people. We would include in such a volume histories by A. J. P. Taylor and Bede, drama by Shakespeare and T. S. Eliot, legends of King Arthur woven into a poem by Tennyson, more poems by Chaucer and Keats, novels by Jane Austen and Sir Walter Scott, essays by Bacon, a diary by Pepys, a parable by John Bunyan, hymns by Montgomery and Isaac Watts, sermons by Wesley and Dale.

So in the Old Testament we may expect to find history and folk-lore, drama and legend, poetry and parable, sermons and hymns.

The Book of Genesis, for instance, opens with a creation poem and contains the folk-lore of the Hebrew people and the beginnings of their national history. Leviticus is a law book. Joshua, Judges, Samuel, Kings, Chronicles, Ezra and Nehemiah are history books. Job is a play. Esther is a historical novel. Ruth is a love story. Jonah is a parable. The Psalms form the hymn book of the nation. The Prophetic works preserve the sermons of the great religious leaders.

Yet although the books of the Old Testament vary considerably in character, they have one thing in common — and that is God.

What then do we mean by the word BIBLE?

It was originally a neuter plural, *Biblia*, which means 'The Books', a word used by Greek writers which passed into the vocabulary of the Western Church. Then in the thirteenth century, the Greek neuter plural came to be regarded as a Latin feminine singular, and 'The Books' became by common consent 'The Bible' (*biblos* singular), in which form the word has passed into the languages of modern Europe.

It is clear, therefore, that if we are to understand the Bible, we should approach it with the help of experts. Scholars have written books called 'commentaries' which will take us verse by verse through each book, showing us meanings we would otherwise miss. You should consult your parish priest for guidance before you choose one of these commentaries because some are more difficult to follow than others.

The Creeds

The writings of the New Testament were written by
Christians of the early Church, and we know that the New
Testament had taken its present shape by AD 367. These
writings vary considerably in what they have to say about
the nature of God and the person of Jesus, and it was
inevitable that people began to differ one from the other in
their understanding of God. This state of things could have
given rise to all sorts of splinter groups, so to prevent this
from happening the Church drew up the Creeds. The
Church quite rightly believed that if the New Testament
had been written by her then she had every right to ensure
that her members interpreted her scriptures correctly.

There are two creeds which concern us directly:

The Apostles Creed
I believe in God the Father Almighty,
Maker of heaven and earth:
And in Jesus Christ his only Son our Lord,
Who was conceived by the Holy Ghost,
Born of the Virgin Mary, Suffered under
Pontius Pilate, Was crucified, dead, and
buried, He descended into hell; The third
day he rose again from the dead, He ascended
into heaven, And sitteth on the right hand
of God the Father Almighty; From thence he
shall come to judge the quick and the dead.
I believe in the Holy Ghost; the holy
Catholick Church; The Communion of Saints;
The Forgiveness of Sins; The Resurrection
of the body, And the life everlasting. Amen.

This Creed grew from the baptismal questions of the early Church and is based on the threefold baptismal command of Jesus — 'Go forth therefore and make all nations my disciples, baptize men everywhere in the name of the Father and the Son and the Holy Spirit' (St Matthew 28 v.19). It is mainly used at the service of Baptism and at Morning and Evening Prayer.

The Nicene Creed

I believe in one God.

The Father Almighty, Maker of heaven and earth, and of all things visible and invisible:

And in one Lord Jesus Christ, the only-begotten Son of God,

Begotten of his Father before all worlds,

God of God, Light of Light, Very God of Very God.

Begotten, not made, being of one substance with the Father, by whom all things were made.

Who for us men, and for our salvation came down from heaven,

And was Incarnate by the Holy Ghost of the Virgin Mary, and was made man.

And was crucified also for us under Pontius Pilate.

He suffered, and was buried.

And the third day he rose again according to the Scriptures,

And ascended into heaven, and sitteth on the right hand of the Father.

And he shall come again with glory to judge both the quick and the dead: whose kingdom shall have no end.

And I believe in the Holy Ghost, the Lord and giver of life,

Who proceedeth from the Father and the Son,

Who with the Father and the Son together is worshipped
and glorified, who spake by the Prophets.
And I believe one holy Catholic and Apostolic Church.
I acknowledge one Baptism for the remission of sins:
And I look for the Resurrection of the dead,
And the Life of the world to come. Amen.

This Creed is used in the service of Holy Communion
and is much more detailed than the Apostles Creed and
traces its origins back to the fourth and fifth centuries.

Some people find it difficult to say the Creeds and wish
that certain statements could be either altered or dropped.
The Creeds, however, are there to safeguard us from
wrongly interpreting the Scriptures.

In a sense, the Statements of the Creeds serve the same
purpose as the laws of a game. Two teams could never
play, shall we say, a game of hockey unless they understood and were in agreement about the laws. The laws of a
game are not negative but positive in that they enable the
game to be played. It is in that sense that we should view
the statements of the Creed; they enable us to interpret the
Scriptures positively and without error. And Christians the
world over who accept the Creed can worship easily
together because they have a common understanding of the
New Testament.

DISREGARD OF THE CREEDS

However, from time to time movements or sects have
sprung up which disregard the Creeds and bend the Scriptures to their own distorted viewpoints, and claim to have a
monopoly of the truth. This has happened on such a wide
scale in America that one could worship with a different
sect on all three hundred and sixty five days of the year!

Let us consider just two of these American sects which
have crept across the Atlantic and see how hopelessly out of

touch they are with what we can call the main stream Christianity.

'The Unification Church' otherwise known as 'The Moonies'

Moonies take their name from the founder of their sect, Sun Myung Moon, who was born in Korea in 1920 and now lives, surrounded by great wealth, in the United States of America. Moon claims to have had a vision when he was sixteen, in which Jesus Christ appeared to him, and asked him to complete the work Jesus had come on earth to do, but which had been cut short by the crucifixion. In 1945 Moon claims to have had another vision in which Jesus Christ bowed down to him and hailed him as his superior. No doubt, as a result of these visions, Moon claims to have the ability of uniquely interpreting the Scriptures and consequently making the absurd statement in a speech he delivered in New Orleans, on 28 October 1973 when he said:

'There can be no doubt that John the Baptist was a man of failure. He was directly responsible for the crucifixion of Jesus Christ.'

This and much else in his teaching contradicts the main stream teaching of world-wide Christianity as enshrined in the Creeds.

The followers of Sun Myung Moon are extremely active in their attempts to win converts to their sect. Often times, on their initial approach they camouflage their true identity by saying that they belong to 'The Unification Church', 'The Holy Spirit Association' or to 'The House Church Association' or to 'The United Family Enterprizes'. It is only later, after a relationship has been established that they reveal their true identity. The Moonies call this method 'Heavenly deception'. Christians should be constantly on guard when approached by such people.

The founder of this sect was a shopkeeper called Charles Taze Russell who was born in Pittsburgh in 1852. He was a 'normal' enough Christian up to the age of twenty when he decided to start his own movement. He was an eloquent speaker and a prolific writer and soon built up a following.

Russell taught that the second though secret coming of Jesus had occurred in 1872 and that the end of the world would occur in 1914. This did not happen! So his followers have postponed the date until 1984. In 1984 Gabriel will blow his trumpet and the Battle of Armageddon will begin when the hosts of God will do battle with the hosts of Satan. The battle will be won by God. Satan and his followers will be dismissed and the 144,000 faithful Jehovah's Witnesses will be taken up into heaven, there to rule with Christ over an earth which will be inhabited by people of good will.

The Jehovah's Witnesses have no love for the Church, Catholic or Protestant; they even believe that the Church is under the supervision and the control of the Devil, and form a part of his visible organization, and therefore constitutes the anti-Christ. Their chief task seems to be knocking on people's doors and trying to persuade people to buy their pamphlets published by the 'Watch Tower Bible and Tract Society'. They are very familiar with certain texts from the Bible and use them to establish their beliefs. But do not be impressed, read St Matthew 4 vv.1–11 or St Luke 4 vv.1–13 and you will see that the Devil himself was able to quote the Scriptures!

The teachings of this sect do not accord with the teaching of the Church, and cannot in any way stand up to the scrutiny of the Creeds.

Sacraments

The word 'sacrament' means an outward visible sign of that which is inward and spiritual. It comes from the Latin word *sacramentum* which means 'a promise'. *Sacramentum* was the promise made by a Roman soldier to his Emperor when he was admitted into the army.

We constantly use sacraments in our every day life. For example: a handshake is an outward and visible sign of friendship which is inward and spiritual; a wedding ring is an outward and visible sign that a person is married; a bank note is an outward, visible sign of a sum of money held by the bank.

The Church has two principal sacraments ordained by Christ himself, viz. Holy Baptism and Holy Communion.

Holy Communion

Holy Baptism

Jesus' words to Nicodemus indicate clearly the importance of baptism: 'In truth I tell you, no one can enter the kingdom of God without being born from water and spirit'. (St John 3. 5)

We can be baptized in two ways. Either by total immersion in water three times, in the name of the Father and of the Son and of the Holy Ghost. Or by having water poured over the brow of the head three times in the name of the Father and of the Son and of the Holy Ghost.

The outward and visible sign in baptism is the use of water in the name of the Trinity; the inward and spiritual is the indwelling of the Holy Spirit within us. St Paul makes this clear in his first letter to the Christians in Corinth when he tells them, 'Surely you know that you are God's temple, where the Spirit of God dwells'. (I Corinthians 3. 16)

It is through baptism that a person is admitted into membership of Christ's Church which is the Body of Christ. St Paul tells us, 'Now you are Christ's body, and each of you a limb or organ of it'. (I Corinthians 12. 27)

St Teresa of Avila develops the theme in her prayer (*see p 56*)

The Blessed Sacrament

The outward and visible signs of this sacrament are bread and wine. The inward and spiritual gifts are the body and blood of Jesus.

This is the central act of Christian worship. This is the supreme act of Christian thanksgiving.

In the New Testament there are four accounts of its institution.

St Paul writes: 'For the tradition which I handed on to you came to me from the Lord himself: that the Lord Jesus on the night of his arrest, took bread and, after giving thanks to God, broke it and said: "This is my body, which is for you; do this as a memorial of me". In the same way, he took the cup after supper, and said: "This cup is the new covenant sealed by my blood. Whenever you drink it, do this as a memorial of me". For every time you eat this bread and drink the cup, you proclaim the death of the Lord, until he comes'. (I Corinthians 11. 23–26)

St Matthew writes: 'During supper Jesus took bread, and having said the blessing he broke it and gave it to the disciples with the words: "Take this and eat; this is my body". Then he took a cup, and having offered thanks to God he gave it to them with the words: "Drink from it, all of you. For this is my blood, the blood of the covenant, shed for many for the forgiveness of sins" '. (St Matthew 26. 26–28)

St Mark writes: 'During supper he took bread, and having said the blessing he broke it and gave it to them, with the words: "Take this; this is my body". Then he took a cup, and having offered thanks to God he gave it to them; and they all drank from it. And he said, "This is my blood, the blood of the covenant, shed for many" '. (St Mark 14. 22–24)

St Luke writes: 'Then he took a cup, and after giving thanks he said, "Take this and share it among yourselves; for I tell you, from this moment I shall drink from the fruit of the vine no more until the time when the kingdom of God comes". And he took bread, gave thanks, and broke it; and he gave it to them, with the words: "This is my body" '. (St Luke 22. 17–19)

We must always bear in mind that the Christian faith flowed out of the Jewish faith and that Jesus and his disciples were Jews. This means that much of the symbolism we find in the New Testament belongs to the Jewish religion, and unless we understand what the Jews believed, we shall not fully understand the teaching of the Cross.

When a Jew sinned he believed that the covenant between himself and God was broken, which meant separation from God. If he wished to repair the broken relationship certain steps were necessary, as laid down in the Book of Leviticus, the great law book of the Bible.

The sinner had to take an unblemished (perfect) lamb, and after laying his hand on the victim's head, slaughter it. The lamb's death wiped away the sin. The priest who was present took some of the lamb's blood and poured it on the base of God's altar; through the blood of the lamb the sinner was made one again with God. (Leviticus 4. 27–30)

The writer of the Letter to the Hebrews explains how Jesus brought this form of sacrifice to its fulfilment, by offering the perfect sacrifice once and for all. Jesus as our priest on Calvary offered his own perfect body on the altar of the cross, his death wiping away our sin, his blood re-uniting us with God. (Hebrews 9. 11–22)

'Offered was he for greatest and for least
Himself the victim, and himself the Priest'.

Before we partake of the Blessed Sacrament, we confess our sins to God and ask for pardon through the perfect sacrifice of Jesus Christ. We are assured of forgiveness and union with God through the body and the blood of Jesus. When we receive the bread we recall that it is through the death of Jesus that our sins are wiped away. When we receive the wine, we remember that it is through the

19

shedding of Jesus's blood that we are re-united with God.

And so we pray: 'O Lamb of God who takest away the sins of the world, have mercy upon us'.

The lamb was also the symbol of deliverance. It was the mark of the blood of a lamb on the doorposts and lintel, which the lamb had to die to provide, which kept the Israelite homes safe on the night of the first Passover. What happened then led to the Jews leaving Egypt and slavery and entering the Promised Land and freedom. (Exodus 12. 1–36)

The service of the Blessed Sacrament is known by four titles: the Holy Communion, the Lord's Supper, the Eucharist and the Mass. Each title lays emphasis on a particular aspect of this service.

The Holy Communion This title means what the words denote — communion or union with our Lord.

The Lord's Supper Our Lord instituted this sacrament during a meal. If our Lord had wanted to demonstrate that he desired to become part of us, he could not have done it more effectively than through the idea of food. The bread and wine become part of us.

The Eucharist This is a Greek word meaning 'thanksgiving', 'joy'. We express our thanksgiving and joy to God for having revealed himself to us; for the 'Gospel', the 'Good News', which tells us that we have immediate access to God through Jesus.

The Mass This word comes from the Latin phrase *Ite, Missa est* which occured at the end of the Roman Catholic service of Holy Communion. It meant that the congregation could go. The people were dismissed. But the meaning behind the word is of paramount importance, it is that of sacrifice. Jesus has offered the perfect and complete sacrifice to God once and for all on our behalf. That is why we are able to obtain God's forgiveness when we ask for it 'through Jesus Christ our Lord'.

Holy Orders

There are three Orders in the Church viz. Bishop, Priest and Deacon.

Bishop

All spiritual authority given to the church is concentrated in the person of the Bishop. He alone can confer Holy Orders and administer the rite of Confirmation. Only a bishop can make (consecrate) a bishop. Only a bishop can make (ordain) a priest. Only a bishop can make a deacon.

A Bishop

Insignia (Badges) of a Bishop

Ring The emblem of fidelity (faithfulness) to the Church. Worn on the third finger of the right hand. Made of gold and usually containing an amethyst.

Mitre (Greek: *Mitra* — Turban). The liturgical head-dress of a bishop. It has been suggested that the two lappets which hang from the back were originally used for tying beneath the chin to prevent the mitre from being blown off.

Pastoral Staff or Crosier The Bishop carries his staff to indicate that he is the chief shepherd of his diocese.

Pectoral Cross (Latin: *Pectus* — Breast). A cross made of precious metal worn on the breast and suspended from the neck by a chain.

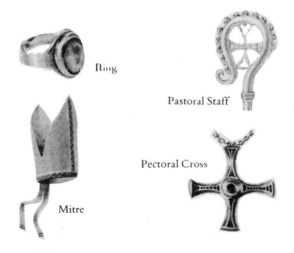

Ring

Pastoral Staff

Pectoral Cross

Mitre

Priest

At his ordination a man is given authority by the Bishop to exercise the authority of a priest. This means that he can celebrate the service of Holy Communion, administer the rite of Baptism, preach the Word, grant absolution of sins, give the blessing, and solemnize Holy Matrimony.

A Priest
(notice how he wears his stole)

Deacon

When a man is made a deacon the Bishop gives him authority to preach the Word and to assist the priest especially at the Holy Communion.

A Deacon
(notice how he wears his stole)

Ordination

Many people are aware early on in their lives that they have special gifts which will determine their careers. The way forward for them is clear cut. They know what they want to do.

Others, on the other hand, experience uncertainty and difficulty as they consider the future, realizing that a wrong choice could mean doing something for the rest of their lives which they will not particularly enjoy.

Whoever we are, we should always discuss the way forward with God asking for his advice and guidance. There is, however, one question we should all ask.

'IS GOD CALLING ME TO BE A PRIEST IN HIS CHURCH?'

If, after giving the matter a lot of thought and prayer, you feel that God is calling you, you should approach your parish priest and talk the matter over with him.

The strength of the Church lies to a great extent in the quality of its priests and it is vital that the Church should have a constant supply of young people of varying gifts offering themselves for the Sacred Ministry.

Confession

Confessing our sins to God should be a regular part of our prayer life, and we can be assured that every sin we confess will be forgiven and wiped away. To doubt this is to doubt the love of God and the very heart of the Christian faith.

There are three ways of confessing our sins:

(i) Privately, when we say our prayers alone;

(ii) Publicly, when we all join together in church and say together the prayer of Confession:

> Almighty God, our heavenly Father,
> we have sinned against you and against our fellow men,
> in thought and word and deed,
> through negligence, through weakness,
> through our own deliberate fault,
> We are truly sorry,
> and repent of all our sins.
> For the sake of your Son Jesus Christ, who died for us,
> forgive us all that is past;
> and grant that we may serve you in newness of life,
> to the glory of your name. Amen.

(iii) Sacramentally, to a priest.

Sometimes we may feel that although we have confessed our sins privately, and even thought of them when we said the prayer of Confession publicly, we still feel unforgiven. Sometimes certain sins we have committed weigh heavily on our consciences and we go around with a constant feeling of guilt. Should this happen to you, you should seek advice from your parish priest and he will either agree to help you himself or put you in touch with another priest. You will then come to the priest and confess your sins to God aloud, and the priest as God's minister will absolve you. He will also help you with spiritual counsel and advice. Remember, whatever you tell a priest in confession will be kept in absolute secrecy.

Someone will say, 'Why won't God let me forget the wrong I have done once he has forgiven me?' The answer is quite simple. Your memory of the sin will act as a signpost so that when you are faced with the same temptation again, you will recall the misery that the sin caused you previously, and this will help you to avoid repeating the same mistake.

Seasons, Feasts and Holy Days

Advent (Latin: *Adventus* — Coming)

The season of Advent covers the four Sundays leading up to Christmas. It is a solemn season when the Church's teaching reminds us that at his Second Coming Jesus will come as our Judge when each one of us will be required to render an account of the way we have lived our lives.

'When the Son of Man comes in his glory and all the angels with him, he will sit in state on his throne, with all the nations gathered before him. He will separate men into two groups, as a shepherd separates the sheep from the goats, and he will place the sheep on his right hand and the goats on his left'. (St Matthew 25. 31–33)

Christmas Day December 25th

The feast day of the birth of Jesus Christ.

'. . . Joseph went up to Judaea from the town of Nazareth in Galilee, to register at the city of David, called Bethlehem, because he was of the house of David by descent; and with him went Mary who was betrothed to him. She was expecting a child, and while they were there the time came for her baby to be born, and she gave birth to a son, her first-born. She wrapped him in his swaddling clothes, and laid him in a manger, because there was no room for them to lodge in the house'. (St Luke 2. 4–7)

Epiphany (Greek: *Epiphaneia* — Showing forth) January 6th

Sometimes known as the Twelfth Day of Christmas. This feast reminds us that Jesus was shown to the Wise Men, the representatives of the non-Jewish world.

> '. . . and the star which they had seen at its rising went ahead of them until it stopped above the place where the child lay. At the sight of the star they were overjoyed. Entering the house, they saw the child with Mary his mother, and bowed to the ground in homage to him; then they opened their treasures and offered him gifts: gold, frankincense, and myrrh'. (St Matthew 2. 9–11)

Ash Wednesday

The first day of Lent, so named after the custom of sprinkling ashes on the heads of the faithful as a token of mourning and penitence.

Lent

An old English word meaning Springtime. Lent is the forty days fast (excluding Sundays) which leads up to Easter.

Maundy Thursday

On the evening before he was crucified, Jesus instituted the service of the Holy Communion in the Upper Room in Jerusalem. Afterwards, according to John, Jesus said to his disciples, 'I give you a new commandment: love one another; as I have loved you, so you are to love one another. If there is this love among you, then all will know that you are my disciples'. (St John 13.34)

The Latin for a new commandment is *mandatum novum*,

and it has been suggested that the word 'Maundy' comes from the Latin *mandatum*.

Good Friday

The day on which Jesus was crucified.

'They brought him to the place called Golgotha, which means 'Place of a skull'. He was offered drugged wine, but he would not take it. Then they fastened him to the cross . . . At midday a darkness fell over the whole land; which lasted till three in the afternoon; and at three Jesus cried aloud, '*Eli, Eli, lama sabachthani*?', which means, 'My God, my God, why hast thou forsaken me?' Some of the bystanders on hearing this, said, 'Hark, he is calling Elijah.' A man ran and soaked a sponge in sour wine and held it to his lips on the end of a cane. 'Let us see', he said, 'if Elijah will come to take him down'. Then Jesus gave a loud cry and died. And the curtain of the temple was torn in two from top to bottom. And when the centurion who was standing opposite him saw how he died, he said, 'Truly this man was a son of God'.' (St Mark 15. 22–24, 33–39)

Easter Day

The feast of the Resurrection of Jesus Christ from the dead.

'Early on the Sunday morning, while it was still dark, Mary of Magdala came to the tomb. She saw that the stone had been moved away from the entrance, and ran to Simon Peter and the other disciple, the one whom Jesus loved. "They have taken the Lord out of his tomb", she cried "and we do not know where they have laid him". So Peter and the other set out and made their way to the tomb. They were running side

31

by side, but the other disciple outran Peter and reached the tomb first. He peered in and saw the linen wrappings lying there, but did not enter. Then Simon Peter came up, following him, and he went into the tomb. He saw the linen wrappings lying, and the napkin which had been over his head, not lying with the wrappings but rolled together in a place by itself. Then the disciple who had reached the tomb first went in too, and he saw and believed; until then they had not understood the scriptures, which showed that he must rise from the dead".' (St John 20. 1–9)

Since Jesus rose from the dead on the first day of the week, Christians have made this their holy day. Sunday is a weekly commemoration of the Resurrection.

According to the Venerable Bede the name Easter comes from the name of the Anglo-Saxon Spring Goddess *Eostre*.

The custom of exchanging Easter eggs is very ancient, and is regarded by some as a symbol of the Resurrection. Just as a chick emerges from the tomb of the egg, so Jesus emerged from his tomb.

Ascension Day

This day occurs forty days after the Resurrection. During these forty days Jesus showed himself on many occasions to his followers:

He showed himself to these men after his death, and gave ample proof that he was alive: over a period of forty days he appeared to them and taught them about the kingdom of God'. (Acts 1. 3)

Ascension Day brought these appearances to a close. Jesus took his disciples on to the Mount of Olives and 'as they watched, he was lifted up, and a cloud removed him from their sight'. (Acts 1.9)

Whit Sunday (Pentecost)

Ten days after the ascension of Jesus into heaven the disciples were gathered together in a room in Jerusalem when the Holy Spirit came upon them. St Luke describes the occasion for us:

'While the day of Pentecost was running its course they were altogether in one place, when suddenly there came from the sky a noise like that of a strong driving wind, which filled the whole house where they were sitting. And there appeared to them tongues like flames of fire, dispersed among them and resting on each one. And they were all filled with the Holy Spirit and began to talk in other tongues, as the Spirit gave them power of utterance'. (Acts 2. 1–4)

Trinity Sunday

The teaching of this day focuses our attention on the central teaching of the Christian faith, that the one God whom we worship exists in three Persons: Father, Son and Holy Ghost.

Trinity (or Sundays after Pentecost)

The season of Trinity covers almost a half of the Church's calendar, during which time the general teaching of the Christian faith is systematically covered.

Retreats

Someone once said that going on retreat was rather like birdwatching. In our daily life, we see birds and hear them, but often we only catch a glimpse of them in flight or a snatch of their song. If we wanted to look at them more closely, and really get to know and recognize their voices, we would need to set aside time when we could become still and attentive, waiting and listening for them. This is what we try to do in prayer: not only to bring to God our active worship and love, our thanks and concerns, but also to be still before him, attentive to his presence and his voice. But sometimes it is difficult to create this inner space of watchful and loving attentiveness to God. The pressures of time, of noise, and of our achievement-oriented society lead us all too easily into a relationship with God in which *we* seem to be the speakers and initiators: 'Don't just stand there, *do* something!'

We must never forget that at the heart of the relationships with all those whom we love is a delight in simply being with them, deepening our friendship not by 'doing' anything, or in any way imposing ourselves on them, but by just 'standing' there, and sharing time and experience together. A retreat is an attempt to deepen our relationship with God by discovering ways of 'standing' before him. Leaving behind our activities, the inner and outer noise, the limitedness of our time, the anxiety, is a way to become free for this discovery. Having stopped, we can look and listen. Our sensitivity to God is sharpened in this 'watching', sometimes by the silence which becomes a 'presence', a silence in which we can know God, and come to learn his searching out and knowing us. Sometimes, awareness is heightened by music or by liturgy, or by exploring ways of meditation. Retreats used to conform to a regular pattern of silence and addresses made by the retreat conductor, but now a varied range of programmes is offered by retreat houses, which provide, in addition, such approaches as Christian yoga and the creative arts. There is also a long tradition of hospitality for individuals seeking a time of quiet and reflection. It is often a deep and enlarging experience to share in the peace and rhythm of a religious community, and many retreat houses are set in beautiful countryside.

A retreat is not a negative 'getting away' so much as a positive "coming to"; to look for the beauty of God's presence, to listen to the richness of his word, and to learn to go forward in his love, the mainspring of all our activities done in his Name.

'Be still, and know that I am God'. (Psalm 46. 10)

The Seven Gifts of the Holy Spirit

Wisdom

That which enables us to see and to understand the true meaning of things and to discover the will of God.

Understanding

That which enables us to see the purpose that lies behind life.

Counsel

That inward voice which directs our thoughts towards God.

Fortitude

That quality which enables us to stand fast under the severest of trials

Knowledge

That which enables us to tell the difference between what is true and what is false.

Piety

That feeling of awe and reverence which we experience in the presence of the majestic and divine which leads us into worship.

Fear of the Lord

That feeling of awe and reverence which deters us from offending God.

The Seven Virtues

Faith

A mixture of conviction, assurance and trust. The passionate belief in a thing which makes a person spend all that he is and has on it.

Hope

The sense of expectancy which floods a person when he realizes that there is a purpose to life.

Charity

That love which reaches out not only to our family and friends but also to our fellow men, even our enemies. It is the power to love the unlovable.

Justice

Fair mindedness. Fair play. Reasonableness.

Prudence

Clear thinking. Far sightedness.

Temperance

Self discipline. Self control.

Fortitude

Steadfastness in the face of the severest trial.

The Seven Deadly Sins

Pride

Arrogant insolence. Big headedness. It appears at its worst when a man defies God and treats his fellow men with contempt.

Lechery

Impurity of thought or word or deed.

Envy

Discontentment and disgruntlement which grips the mind when we desire what others have.

Anger

It has been described as a 'brief insanity'. When anger takes over we lose our sense of judgement.

Covetousness

Greed, selfishness. A covetous person is a grasping person.

Gluttony

Over indulgence. A glutton is someone who never knows when he has had enough.

Sloth

Laziness. Bone idleness. A slothful person is someone who does not like work.

Some Words
We Should Know

Absolution A declaration of the forgiveness of sin.

Agnostic An agnostic is open to be convinced about the existence of God, but requires absolute proof. He states that unless something can be demonstrated to be true, it cannot be accepted.

Apostle An ambassador. One who is sent. When Jesus sent his disciples into the world to preach the Gospel, they became Apostles.

Atheist An atheist does not accept the existence of God. To him the term 'God' is meaningless.

Atonement AT-ONE-MENT. When we sin we separate ourselves from God. Through forgiveness of that sin we are made one with God. When Jesus died for us he provided us with the way to obtain at-one-ment with God.

Blessing The authoritative pronouncement of God's favour. Its inner meaning is 'happiness' or 'joy'. When we hear the priest saying 'The blessing of God Almighty, the Father, the Son, and the Holy Spirit be among you, and remain with you always', he is conferring on you God's happiness.

Christ A Greek word meaning 'Anointed One'. The Hebrew word for 'Anointed One' is 'Messiah'.

Church From a Greek word describing something which belongs to God and which was applied originally to a church building. It also, and more importantly, means the gathered people of God.

Covenant An agreement. A bargain. A testament.

Disciple A follower.

Glory Reflection. To glorify means to reflect. To reflect in pure joy the love of God is to glorify him. We glorify God when we praise him. We glorify God when we reflect his love towards our fellow beings.

Gospel GODSPEL — an old English word which means 'GOOD NEWS'.

Grace A free and unearned gift from God. A gift which transforms us into creatures of spiritual loveliness.

Holy Separated. Set apart for God.

Incarnation This teaching states that Jesus the Son of God took human flesh from his human mother.

Jesus This is the Greek form of the Hebrew name JOSHUA, which means 'God saves'.

Liturgy This word has two uses:
1. To describe all the authorized services of the Church.
2. Specifically as a title for the service of the Holy Communion.

Mercy Sympathy. A merciful person is someone who not only feels sorry about another's suffering but also has the ability to get inside that person's situation.

Miracle An act of divine power breaking through from the spiritual world into the physical world.

Parable A story drawn from nature or from human affairs, used to convey a spiritual truth.

Reconcile To heal a broken friendship.

Redeem To buy back something which originally belonged to you.

Repent To feel sorry about something.

Saint A person who has been officially recognized by the Church as having achieved great holiness. Strictly speaking, however, everyone who has been baptized into the Church of Christ and who is therefore 'in Christ' is a saint.

Salvation Deliverance from the power of sin and its consequences.

Sin An offence against God.

Soul That part of man which survives his physical death and returns to God.

Testament Agreement. Covenant. Instead of talking about 'the Old Testament' and 'the New Testament' we could say instead 'the Old Agreement' and 'the New Agreement'.

The Church's Colours

The red, green and amber of traffic lights control the flow of traffic because motorists understand what these colours mean. Similarly the green/yellow, brown and blue wires in an electric cable indicate which wire is earth, live and neutral.

The Church has used colours since the 12th Century to tell the faithful the sort of mood she is in. There are four principal colours, viz violet, white, red and green.

When the Church wears:

Violet she is in a solemn mood. Violet is the colour of penitence and is used particularly for the seasons of Advent (the four weeks before Christmas), and Lent (the forty days before Easter).

White she is in a happy and festive mood.

Red she is commemorating the death of someone who shed his blood for the Faith. We call these people martyrs. Red is also the colour used on Whitsunday, because it symbolizes the tongues of fire.

Green she is in a natural mood. Green is the colour of nature and is used during the seasons of Epiphany and Trinity.

The Government of the Church

Before anyone can nominate a person for any office in the Church of England, or vote for any person, or stand for any office in the Church of England, he must have his name entered on the Electoral Roll of a parish. To do this a person must be baptized, at least sixteen years old, and either resident in the parish or a habitual worshipper in it for at least six months, and must have applied in proper form.

Once a person has his name entered on the roll, he can at once stand for election on to the Parochial Church Council.

Deanery Synod The Deanery Synod is made up of the clergy of the Rural Deanery together with elected lay members from each parish.

Diocesan Synod This is made up of the Bishop, and elected clergy and lay persons from each Deanery Synod.

General Synod This is the Parliament of the Church where Church policy and teaching is decided. Elections to the General Synod are conducted at deanery level and not as one might have expected at diocesan level. This system ensures that there is a direct link between the General Synod and the parish.

The Officers of the Church

Archbishop When the bishops of a Province meet, the Archbishop, as the senior bishop, takes the Chair.

Bishop The Bishop is the chief shepherd of the flock and is recognized as such by the shepherd's staff he carries in his hand. He is the Father in God to the clergy and people of his diocese and also the chief administrator of the diocese.

Dean The Dean ranks next to the Bishop in the Cathedral, but is usually considerably independent of the Bishop. He is the chairman of that body of clergy which serves the cathedral and is called the Cathedral Chapter. The Chapter is responsible for the maintenance of the Cathedral and its services.

Provost Where the Cathedral is also a parish church, the head of the Cathedral Chapter is called the Provost. He enjoys the precedence and dignity of a dean.

Canon A canon is a member of the Cathedral Chapter.

Precentor In Cathedrals the Precentor is the clergyman responsible for the direction of the choral services.

Archdeacon The Archdeacon is responsible for an area of the diocese called an archdeaconry. In this area he is 'the eyes of the bishop'. His duties vary widely. He keeps in very close touch with the clergy in his archdeaconry, he inspects the fabric of the parish churches and parsonage houses. He normally inducts parish priests to parishes and admits church-wardens to their offices.

Rural Dean The Rural Dean cares for the clergy in a deanery, which is usually made up of about ten parishes. He summons the clergy together for worship, study and fellowship, and is their counsellor and adviser. He acts as the channel of communication between the bishop and the clergy.

Rector In some parishes the parish priest is called the Rector. His predecessors received the revenues of the parish known as tithes which made up the income of the priest.

Vicar In some parishes the parish priest is called the Vicar. Before the Reformation many parishes belonged to monasteries. The monastery received the revenues of the parish and paid a priest to look after the spiritual needs of the parish on its behalf. Such a priest was called a vicar.

Today a clergyman is paid from a central fund, so the difference between a rector and a vicar has no significance.

Curate A clergyman who assists a rector or a vicar in a parish. Formerly the title referred to any clergyman who had charge ('cure') of a parish.

Chancellor The Chancellor is the legal official of a diocese, and is not usually an ordained person.

Churchwardens There are usually two Churchwardens. These are elected each year at the Easter Vestry. The Churchwardens are not officers of the Bishop; their main duties are to oversee the finances of the church and to care for its fabric and furnishings.

Parochial Church Councillors These are elected at an annual meeting of those church members aged eighteen years and over whose names appear on the Electoral Roll of the parish. Parochial Church Councillors meet as a body at least four times a year and co-operate with the parish priest in the running of church matters.

Sidespeople These are usually appointed at the annual meeting of the church. They assist the wardens in the collection of alms, and in larger churches help with the seating of the congregation.

Reader A Reader is a person, not in Holy Orders, who has been licensed by the Bishop to conduct religious services, preach sermons, read the Epistle at the Communion Service and administer the chalice.

Verger A Verger is to be found in cathedrals and large churches. Strictly speaking, he is the official who carries a mace or 'verge' before a dignitary e.g. the Bishop or the Dean, when in procession.

A Cathedral

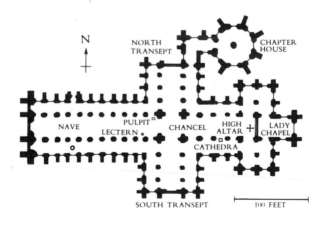

N

NORTH TRANSEPT

CHAPTER HOUSE

NAVE

PULPIT

LECTERN

CHANCEL

HIGH ALTAR

CATHEDRA

LADY CHAPEL

SOUTH TRANSEPT

100 FEET

Altar A table made of wood or stone, consecrated by a bishop, on which the bread and wine is placed for the celebration of the Holy Communion.

Cathedra The bishop's chair or throne. A church which contains the *cathedra* is known as a cathedral.

Chancel The area within the main body of the church east of the nave and transepts, usually reserved for the clergy and choir.

Font A large bowl-shaped object which holds the water used in baptism.

Lady Chapel A chapel dedicated to the Blessed Virgin Mary ('Our Lady'). It is frequently to be found in one of the transepts.

Lectern A stand made of brass or wood on which the Bible rests. Sometimes the lectern takes the shape of a bird with outstretched wings standing on a ball. The ball represents the world, the bird symbolizes the Word of God being carried to all parts.

Nave That part of a church where the people sit. The term is generally thought to come from the Latin word, *navis*, a ship. Christians from early times have thought of the church as being a ship which carries them safely across the seas of life.

A Bishop's Chair (Cathedra)
from Saxon Times
(Beverley Minster)

Pulpit Where sermons are preached.

Transept The north and south transepts are like arms which stand at right angles to the nave giving the church the shape of a cross.

A Bishop's Chair
(Cathedra) with Canopy
(Exeter Cathedral)

The World Wide Church

The population of the world is about 3000 million; of this number, it is estimated that 1000 million are Christians. This means that one-third of the world's population is Christian. How does this compare with the three other world religions?

Hinduism — 370 million
Buddhism — 300 million
Islam   — 400 million

At present Christianity is not expanding in Britain or in Europe, but consider the following information.

In the United States in 1910 about 40 per cent of the population was Christian. In 1950 it was estimated that 60 per cent was Christian. By 1976 the figure had increased to 77 per cent.

In Africa it is estimated that there are over 100 million Christians and the number is increasing at such a rate that the historian Stephen Neill states that 'on the most sober estimate by the twentieth century, Africa south of the Sahara will be in the main a Christian continent'.

Latin America has been a Christian continent for centuries but in Brazil the Christian church is growing more rapidly than the population.

In South Korea there are 3 million Christians out of a population of 31 million, and this number is increasing at the rate of 10 per cent per year — more than four times as fast as the population growth.

In Burma Christianity was said to be growing in such a way that, in 1972, a new church was being organized every week.

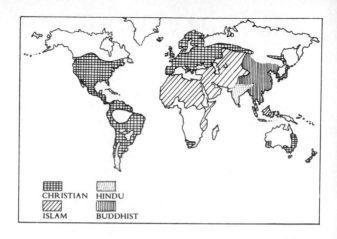

CHRISTIAN   HINDU
ISLAM   BUDDHIST

In Indonesia the number of Christians is said to have increased from 4 million in 1964, to 8 million in 1970.

In India, by 1974, it was estimated that there were 14 million Christians.

It is clear from this picture that the Christian Church is very much on the march. Things are happening on a global scale. But there are millions of Christians in some of these countries who are desperately poor, who live out their lives under wretched conditions. The church in the wealthier parts of the world is extremely conscious of this and sends help through its missionary societies.

Your local church in every probability supports one or more of these societies and depends absolutely on your generosity.

PRAYERS

Give us O God:
    Thoughts which turn into prayer,
    Prayer which turns into love,
    Love which turns into deeds
                    Amen.

The Lord's Prayer

Our Father, who art in heaven,
hallowed be thy name;
thy kingdom come;
thy will be done;
on earth as it is in heaven.
Give us this day our daily bread.
And forgive us our trespasses,
as we forgive those who trespass against us.
And lead us not into temptation;
but deliver us from evil.
For thine is the kingdom,
the power, and the glory,
for ever and ever.

                    Amen.

St Benedict

O gracious and Holy Father,
Give us wisdom to see thee,
intelligence to understand thee,
diligence to seek thee,
patience to wait for thee,
eyes to behold thee,
a heart to meditate upon thee,
and a life to proclaim thee,
through the power of the Spirit of
Jesus Christ our Lord.

Amen.

St Francis

Lord, make us instruments of thy peace.
  Where there is hatred, let us sow love;
  Where there is injury, pardon;
  Where there is discord, union;
  Where there is doubt, faith;
  Where there is despair, hope;
  Where there is darkness, light;
  Where there is sadness, joy;
O Divine Master, grant that we may not so much seek
to be consoled as to console;
to be understood as to understand;
to be loved, as to love;
through the love of thy Son who died for us, Jesus Christ
our Lord.

Amen.

St Ignatius Loyola

Teach us, good Lord
To serve thee as thou deservest;
To give and not to count the cost;
To fight and not to heed the wounds;
To toil and not to seek for rest;
To labour and not to ask for any reward,
Save that of knowing that we do thy will.

Amen.

St Patrick

Christ be with me, Christ within me,
Christ behind me, Christ before me,
Christ beside me, Christ to win me,
Christ to comfort and restore me.
Christ beneath me, Christ above me,
Christ in quiet, Christ in danger,
Christ in heart of all that love me,
Christ in mouth of friend and stranger.

Amen.

St Richard of Chichester

Day by day, dear Lord, of thee
Three things we pray:
To see thee more clearly;
To love thee more dearly;
To follow thee more nearly;
Day by day.

Amen.

St Teresa of Avila

Christ has no body now
   on earth but yours.
No hands but yours,
Yours are the eyes
   through which is to look out
Christ's compassion to the World;
Yours are the feet
   with which he is
to go about doing good;
Yours are the hands
   with which he is
to bless us now.

Amen.

Sir Francis Drake

O Lord God, when thou givest to thy servants to endeavour any great matter, grant us also to know that it is not the beginning, but the continuing of the same unto the end, until it be thoroughly finished, which yieldeth the true glory: through him who for the finishing of thy work laid down his life, our Redeemer, Jesus Christ. *Amen.*

Charles Kingsley

Take from us, O God,
All pride and vanity,
All boasting and forwardness;
And give us the true courage that shows itself by
    gentleness,
The true wisdom that shows itself by simplicity,
And the true power that shows itself by modesty;
Through Jesus Christ our Lord.

                             Amen.

Reinhold Niebuhr

O God, give us
    Serenity to accept what cannot be changed;
    Courage to change what should be changed;
    And wisdom to distinguish the one from the other;
    Through Jesus Christ our Lord.   *Amen*

Courage

O God we pray thee for courage to face unpopularity for the sake of truth; for courage to declare boldly our convictions, though they make us despised; for courage to break with evil custom and evil opinions. Give us strong hearts that will not fear what any person can do to us, or say about us. Give us, O Lord, the spirit of boldness, that being delivered from all fear of our fellows, we may be strong in thee, and very courageous.

Amen

(J. S. HOYLAND, *adapted*)

Good People

For all who have laboured and suffered for freedom, good government, just laws, and happy homes; and for all who have sought to bless men by their generosity and sacrifice in good works, and to lighten the dark places of the earth: We praise thee, O God, and bless thy name. *Amen*.

Grace

O Lord, give us clean hands, clean words, and clean thoughts. Help us to stand for the hard right against the easy wrong. Save us from habits that harm. Teach us to work as hard and play as fair in your sight alone as if all the world saw. Forgive us when we are unkind, and help us to forgive those who are unkind to us. Keep us ready to help others though at cost to ourselves. Send us chances to do a little good every day and so to grow more like Christ.

Amen.

Great Things and Little Things

Lord of infinite greatness, who hast ordered and adorned in equal perfection all that thou hast made; who hast set in glorious array the eternal heavens, and yet dost paint the lily that abideth but a day: Give us courage to attempt great things in thy Name, and equal faithfulness to do the small; to thy sole honour and glory, through Jesus Christ our Lord.

Amen.

Humility

O Father, give us the humility which
   Realizes its ignorance,
   Admits its mistakes,
   Recognizes its need,
   Welcomes advice,
   Accepts rebuke.
Help us always
   To praise rather than to criticize,
   To sympathize rather than to condemn,
   To encourage rather than to discourage,
   To build rather than to destroy,
   And to think of people at their best rather
   than at their worst.
This we ask for thy name's sake.

Amen

(WILLIAM BARCLAY)

Mankind

O God, Father of all mankind, we think before thee this
day of all thy children —
  the people of Europe, with their rich treasures of
  the past, their knowledge and skill, and their great
  hope for the future —
  the people of Asia, with their ageless wisdom and
  their great new ventures —
  the people of Africa, with their warm hearts and their
  open minds, ready for a new destiny —
  the people of America, with their life and vigour,
  their generous hearts, and their pioneering spirit —
  and the people of Australasia, forward looking, strong
  and free.
O Lord, we praise thee for all the infinite variety of
mankind.
Teach us, by thy mercy, how we thy children can learn to
live in unity, according to thy will. For Jesus' sake.

Amen.

(SENIOR TEACHER'S ASSEMBLY BOOK)

Myself

God be in my head,
And in my understanding:
God be in mine eyes,
And in my looking:
God be in my mouth,
And in my speaking:
God be in my heart,
And in my thinking:
God be at my end,
And at my departing.

Amen.

Our Homes

Lord God Almighty, Father of every family, against
whom no door can be shut: Enter into the homes of our
land, we beseech thee, with the angel of thy presence, to
hallow them in pureness and beauty of love; make them
sanctuaries of thy presence and dwelling places of thy love;
and grant to those who are near and dear to us the gentle
ministry and protection of thy Holy Spirit. In the name of
Jesus Christ our Lord.

Amen.

Peace in the World

Eternal God, in whose perfect kingdom no sword is drawn but the sword of righteousness, and no strength known but the strength of love: We pray thee so mightily to shed and spread abroad thy Spirit, that all peoples and ranks may be gathered under one banner, of the Prince of Peace; as children of one God and Father of all, to whom be dominion and glory now and for ever.

Amen.

Perception

O God, when we look about us for
evidence of your presence, open
our minds so that we may see you in:
    the Geometry of the rainbow;
    the Arithmetic of gravity;
    the Physics of the thunder cloud;
    the Chemistry of a raindrop;
    the Engineering of a cobweb;
    the Navigation of migratory birds.
We ask this in the name of Jesus Christ
our Lord.

Amen.

The Gifts of the Holy Spirit

Strengthen us, O Lord, with the Holy Spirit, the
Comforter; and daily increase in us your many gifts
of grace:
    the Spirit of wisdom and understanding,
    the Spirit of counsel and inward strength.
    the Spirit of knowledge and true godliness,
and fill us, Lord, with the spirit which instils
respect for you, now and for ever.

Amen.

The Good Life

    Whatsoever things are true and just;
    Whatsoever things are pure and lovely;
    Whatsoever things are gentle and generous,
        honourable and of good report:
    These things, O Lord, grant that we may
    with one accord pursue, for Jesus Christ's
    sake.

Amen.

The Sick

Holy Father, holy God we commend into thy safe
keeping all those who are sick and in pain.
Be with them in dark hours to comfort them, to
support them and to speak peace to their souls.
Grant to each one a happy issue out of his
affliction. And give to all those who care for
the sick, wisdom and skill, sympathy and patience.
These things we ask in the name of Jesus Christ our
Lord.   *Amen.*

The Tongue

Set a watch upon our tongue, O Lord, that we may never
speak the cruel word which is untrue; or, being true, is not
the whole truth; or, being wholly true, is merciless; for the
love of Jesus Christ our Lord. *Amen.*

Relationships

O Lord, we beseech thee to grant us sensitivity in all our
dealings with each other. Keep us from unkind words and
unkind silences. Make us quick to understand the needs and
feelings of others, and grant that, living in the brightness of
thy presence, we may bring sunshine into cloudy places.

Amen.

(HYMNS AND PRAYERS FOR DRAGONS)

Silence

O Lord, the Scripture says: 'There is a time for silence and a time for speech'. Saviour, teach me the silence of humility, the silence of wisdom, the silence of love, the silence of perfection, the silence that speaks without words, the silence of faith.

Lord, teach me to silence my own heart that I may listen to the gentle movement of the Holy Spirit within me and sense the depths which are of God.   *Amen.*

(FRANKFURT PRAYER — *sixteenth century,*
translated by B. G.)

True Ambition

Eternal and ever-blessed God, equip us, not
only to see, but also to attain the ideal.
    Help us never to be satisfied
    With words without deeds;
    With plans without performance;
    With schemes without results;
    With dreams without toil to make the dreams
come true; that we may follow in the footsteps
of our Lord and Master, Jesus Christ.   *Amen.*

(WILLIAM BARCLAY)

Watchers of the Night

We thank thee, heavenly Father, for those who remain
awake whilst men sleep.
For doctors and nurses who man the hospitals of our
land, relieving pain and comforting the anxious;
For policemen on their lonely patrols, keeping
law and order in our society;
For firemen, standing by, ready to rush out to any
emergency;
For those who keep the lines of communication open
and the wheels of industry turning.   *Amen.*

Contemplation

Thou alone art the taste of my tongue,
Thou art my tongue, ears and eyes,
Thou art the soul within my body; thou art my mind;
Yea, thou art my all in all.
Thou dwellest alone in my heart, and in my breath;
Thou art the life within my body.
Thou fillest my whole body from head to foot;
Thou fillest my heart like water.
I have none but thee. Thou alone art the life within me.

(DADER, *Hindu*)

The Creator

Our God, we recognize in you the master-mind behind all
being, behind the universe. We thank you for the designed
pattern of order and relationships in the far distant galaxies
and in the atom itself. We thank you, not only for the
pattern behind the universe, but for the plan behind the
pattern and the purpose behind the plan. We thank you not
only for the mind that planned but for the love that gave
and revealed the plan. We thank you for the mind becom-
ing man in Christ, and for the purpose beyond space and
time that has reached us through him. In whose name we
offer you these our thanksgivings.

Amen.

(DAVID INGRAM)

Thanksgiving

We thank thee, O Father, for the sun that warms us, and the air that gives us life; for all the beauty of earth, in field and hedgerow, brook and covert, woods and hills; for the changing seasons, each in its order beautiful; for happy homes and cheerful faces; for health and vigour of body and mind; for the food that makes us strong; for this good Britain, the land we love; for freedom and just laws; for the lives and examples of the good and brave of every age and every race; and for the life on earth of Jesus our example, who came to show us how to live. *Amen.*

(HYMNS AND PRAYERS FOR DRAGONS)

Personal

When the heart is hard and parched up, come upon me
    with a shower of mercy.
When grace is lost from life, come with a burst of song.
When tumultuous work raises its din on all sides,
    shutting me out from beyond, come to me, my
    Lord of silence, with thy peace and rest.
When my beggarly heart sits crouched, shut up in a
    corner, break open the door, my king, and come
    with the ceremony of a king.
When desire blinds the mind with delusion and dust,
    O thou holy one, thou wakeful, come with thy
    light and with thy thunder.

(RABINDRATH TAGORE, *1861–1941*, *Gitanjali*)

When in Difficulties

Heavenly Father, be with us during the difficult
times of life.
   Be with us:
   When darkness seems to enter our minds;
   when we are faced with illness;
   when we are misunderstood and let down by
   our friends and loved ones;
   when we are shattered by disappointment;
   when life seems to lose its meaning and
   we become depressed;
   when we are frightened by the thoughts of
   what tomorrow may bring.
Reassure us with your presence, O God, and let
us remember that, where you are, no ill can come.
We ask these things in the name of Jesus Christ
our Lord.

Amen.

To be Like Jesus

Jesus, Friend of the friendless,
Helper of the poor,
Healer of the sick,
Whose life was spent in doing good,
Let us follow in your footsteps;
Make us loving in all our words,
Generous in all our deeds;
Make us strong to do right
Gentle with the weak,
And kind to all who are in sorrow;
That we may be like you,
Our Lord and Master.

Amen.

An Evening Prayer

O Lord, support us all the day long of this pilgrim life, until the shades lengthen and the evening comes, and the busy world is hushed, and the fever of life is over, and our work is done. Then, Lord, in thy mercy, grant us safe lodging, a holy rest, and peace at the last, through Jesus Christ our Lord.

Amen.

An Unknown Saint's Evening Prayer

O God, who hast drawn over the weary day the restful veil of night, enfold us in thy heavenly peace. Lift from our hands our tasks, and all through the night bear in thy bosom the full weight of our burdens and sorrows, that in untroubled slumber we may press our weariness close to thy strength, and win new power for the morrow's duties from thee who givest to thy beloved in sleep: through Jesus Christ our Lord.

Amen.

FOR FURTHER READING

How the Church began. Reginald H. Copestake
How the Church grew. Reginald H. Copestake
Learning about the Church of England. Michael Smith
Learning about Baptism. Neville B. Cryer
Learning about Jesus. Arthur L. Moore
Learning about the Holy Spirit. G. C. B. Davies
Learning about the Resurrection. G. C. B. Davies
Learning to Pray. Michael Turnbull
What is the Bible? Neville B. Cryer
Learning about the Psalms. Frank Colquhoun
Learning about Private Prayer. Desmond B. Tillyer
Learning about Retreats. Sr Joanna Baldwin, Dss, CSA
Learning about the Unification Church (the Moonies). Maurice Burrell
Learning about Jehovah's Witnesses. Maurice Burrell
Learning about the Mormons. Maurice Burrell

(The above titles are published in Mowbray's Enquirer's Library series of 32pp booklets)